Q and A

The little book of questions on....

MARZIPAN SWEETS

Copyright © 2013 Two Magpies Publishing
An imprint of Read Publishing Ltd
Home Farm, 44 Evesham Road, Cookhill, Alcester, Warwickshire, B49 5LJ

Commissioning Editor Rose Hewlett
Words by Sophie Berry
Design and Illustrations by Zoë Horn Haywood

This book is copyright and may not be reproduced or copied in any way without the express permission of the publisher in writing.

British Library Cataloguing-in-Publication Data A catalogue record for this book is available from the British Library.

CONTENTS

Introduction	3
History	7
Equipment	21
Preparation	31
- Cup Measurements	33
- Sugar Stages	37
Basic Recipes	47
Sweet Recipies	59
Top Tips and Tricks	
- Preparation of marzipan sweets	90
- Shaping and crafting	92

INTRODUCTION

THE SKY REALLY IS THE LIMIT WITH MARZIPAN

Making marzipan is a fascinating craft and turning a modest selection of ingredients into delicious sweets can turn a kitchen novice into an eager cook.

The beauty of marzipan is that once you have mastered a basic recipe you can add whatever food colouring you wish, flavour it with any essence you like, and mold it into countless shapes. The sky really is the limit with marzipan, and the array of sweets you can make from a base marzipan recipe makes it an extremely versatile confectionery to perfect.

Another upside of making your own marzipan sweets is that you can be sure to use the best and purest ingredients. In an age which tends to be increasingly synthetic, knowing exactly what has gone into your lovingly created confectionery is an attractive prospect.

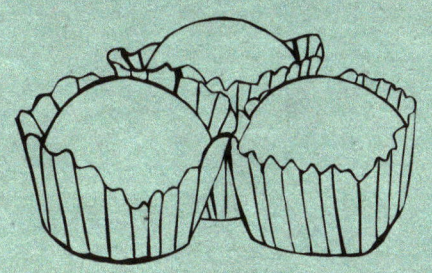

Hopefully you are now feeling inspired to get started on your first batch. This little book will introduce you to a handful of basic marzipan recipes which you can then develop and customise to your liking. The book also details recipes which you can use to create a whole host of marzipan sweets.

This book will endeavour to answer any questions you have about art of making marzipan, and the methods you can master to craft the most beautiful sweets.

ALL THAT'S LEFT TO SAY IS –
GOOD LUCK!

19TH CENTURY MARZIPAN MOULD!

HISTORY

Q. When was marzipan first made?

A. It is very difficult to trace the origins of marzipan. Versions of the nut-based confectionery appear all over the world, and marzipan sweets have been crafted by generations of cooks.

Q. Where did early versions of marzipan originate?

A. Some say that the original recipe for marzipan came from China, and came to be popular in Europe by travelling through the Medieval Muslim state, Al-Adalus.

Q. Where is Al-Adalus?

A. Al-Adalus was made up of parts of what are now Spain, France, Portugal and Gibraltar.

Q. Where else was early marzipan made?

A. Early marzipan recipes also came from Persia, and made it to Europe via Turkey.

Q. Do any other countries have their own recipes?

A. Königsberg in Prussia is also renowned for it's marzipan manufacturing. Königsberg marzipan refers to a specific type of marzipan which has a burnt top, and added candied fruit.

Q. Is that it?

A. Sicily is another place where marzipan has been made for hundreds of years, and panis martius, or 'March bread' as it is called there, is a traditional Sicilian confectionery.

Q. What is marzipan made from?

A. Marzipan is traditionally made from almonds.

Q. I've heard almonds are good for the heart? Is this true?

A. Almonds are among the most nutritious nuts. They are high in monounsaturated fats, which will help you keep your heart healthy and are good for your skin.

Q. Do almonds have any other health benefits?

A. Yes. They also contain lots of of fibre and protein and are especially high in manganese, magnesium, copper, calcium, iron, zinc, vitamin E and vitamin B2.

Q. So is all marzipan made from almonds?

A. No. You can find other versions of marzipan made from other nuts, and even peach and apricot kernels.

Q. Do the other varieties of marzipan have different names?

A. You may come across something called parzipan, which is marzipan made from peach or apricot kernels. We have included a recipe for parzipan in this book, so keep an eye out for it.

Q. Will I need lots of specialist equipment?

A. No. Equipment is simple. If you want to try a cooked marzipan recipe, you'll need a heavy saucepan, preferably a copper-bottom jam boiler.

Q. How big should the pan be that I use?

A. It must be big enough to hold twice the bulk you are likely to need – boiling sugar bubbles expand a lot.

Q. Will I need a thermometer?

A. Yes, a thermometer is essential. A sugar-boiling thermometer with the various stages marked will be very useful if you would like to try making cooked marzipan.

Q. What about equipment for uncooked marzipan recipes?

A. You will need a couple of large mixing bowls.

Q. What about utensils?

A. You'll need a wooden spoon for stirring, a hand whisk, a rolling pin, pastry brush, and a sharp knife.

Q. Anything else?

A. Some recipes require the marzipan mixture to be kneaded by hand, and a marble slab would be very useful for this. However, any smooth, heat-safe work surface or board is perfect. Storing your board in the fridge before use is a good idea, as it will help the mixture to cool as it is worked.

Q. Is that it?

A. You could invest in some cookie cutters if you'd like to roll and cut out your marzipan into shapes. Cling film will also be useful if you wish to wrap and refrigerate your marzipan to use at a later date.

COOKIE CUTTERS

PREPARATION

Q. Most of the recipes I have seen use cups as a measurement. How much is a cup?

A. A small coffee cup is the best kind to use, and make sure you use the same cup to measure all your ingredients.

Of course, you don't have to use cups - this table is a handy tool if you need to convert cups into other amounts.

CUP MEASURMENTS

1 cup	8 fluid ounces	½ pint	237 ml
2 cups	16 fluid ounces	1 pint	474 ml
4 cups	32 fluid ounces	1 quart	946 ml
2 pints	32 fluid ounces	1 quart	0.946 l
4 quarts	128 fluid ounces	1 gallon	3.784 l

Q. What is the best way to test the temperature of the mixture when making cooked marzipan?

A. A thermometer is the best way to accurately test the temperature of marzipan mixture as it cooks.

Q. Can I tell if my marzipan mixture is cooked without using a thermometer?

A. If you don't have a thermometer, you can determine the temperature of your mixture with the Drop Test, which is when you drop a little mixture into cold water.

Q. What should the mixture look like when its dropped into cold water?

A. Most of the cooked marzipan recipes in this book will state to heat the mixture to soft ball, or firm ball stage stage. However, this does vary so check the recipe carefully before you start.

Have a look at the Drop Test table here for more information on monitoring the temperature of your marzipan mixture without a thermometer.

SUGAR STAGES

STAGE when the mixture is tested in cold water	TEMPERATURE	USES
THREAD Forms a thin liquid thread	110 to 112 °C (230 to 234 °F)	Sugar Syrups
SOFT BALL Forms a soft flexible ball that can be flattened	112 to 116 °C (234 to 241 °F)	Fudge, pralines, fondant and butter creams
FIRM BALL Forms a firm ball that will hold its shape but is still malleable	118 to 120 °C (244 to 248 °F)	Caramel Candies
HARD BALL Forms thick threads from spoon and creates a hard ball that will hold its shape	121 to 130 °C (250 to 266 °F)	Nougat, marshmallows, gummies, and divinity
SOFT CRACK Forms firm flexible threads	132 to 143 °C (270 to 289 °F)	salt water taffy
HARD CRACK Forms hard brittle threads that snap easily	146 to 154 °C (295 to 309 °F)	toffee, brittles, hard candy, and lollipops
CLEAR LIQUID Liquid will begin to change colour. Colour ranges from golden brown to amber	160 °C (320 °F)	caramelised sugar, caramel
BROWN LIQUID Liquid will begin to change colour. Colour ranges from golden brown to amber	170 °C (338 °F)	caramelised sugar, caramel

Q. Does marzipan mixture require kneading, or working?

A. Lots of recipes for marzipan, both cooked and uncooked will require you to work or knead the mixture by hand.

Q. How do you do this?

A. Kneading marzipan is like kneading dough of any kind, like bread or cookie dough for example. You simply push the mixture away from you using the heel of your hand, fold the edges back into the centre and repeat until the dough is smooth.

Q. What if the mixture is hot?

A. If you are trying out a cooked marzipan recipe, make sure you leave the mixture to cool slightly before handling it. Latex gloves will help protect your hands from the heat, too.

Q. Why is this method used?

A. Kneading is a good way to blend your ingredients thoroughly, and some people believe it gives your marzipan a smoother texture.

Q. How do you shape marzipan mixture?

A. There are two simple ways to shape marzipan. The easiest method is to roll your mixture out on a smooth work surface, and use cookie cutters to cut out small shapes.

Q. What is the other method?

A. The other method is to shape your mixture by hand. This is a little bit more time consuming, but allows you to be really creative and make anything you like.

Q. Is this difficult?

A. No, this is very simple, and also rather fun! There are some step-by-step guides on how to mold marzipan into certain shapes in this book which should start you off.

Q. Is marzipan mixture safe for children to handle, and shape?

A. Definitely. Children will love shaping and molding marzipan. Ensure you make an uncooked version so there is no danger of little fingers being burned on hot mixture.

BASIC RECIPIES

Q. Is there a really straightforward marzipan recipe suitable for beginners that I can try making at home?

A. Try this recipe for uncooked marzipan. It is really straight forward and you won't need a thermometer.

CLASSIC UNCOOKED MARZIPAN

INGREDIENTS

½ cup confectioners' sugar
½ cup granulated sugar
2 cups ground almonds
2 egg whites
¼ tsp flavouring (optional)
¼ tsp colouring (optional)

METHOD

1. In a large bowl, sift together the sugar then add the almonds and mix well.
2. Beat the egg whites until they are frothy, and fold them into the sugar and almond mixture.
3. Add the extract and colouring, and knead well to create a stiff paste. Add a little extra sugar if the mixture is too wet.
4. Allow the mixture to stand for a few hours, then press small pieces into molds, or shape by hand. You can also roll the marzipan out flat on a cool work surface powdered with icing sugar and use cutters to shape.
5. Use the marzipan as soon as possible as it won't store for longer than 24 hours.

Q. Is there a simple recipe for cooked marzipan I can try out at home?

A. Yes. This cooked marzipan recipe is very simple, and a good place to start if you're a beginner.

SIMPLE BOILED MARZIPAN

INGREDIENTS

1 lb granulated sugar
½ cup water
2 cups ground almonds
1 tbsp glucose
1 tsp almond flavouring
½ cup icing sugar

METHOD

1. In a large saucepan over a low heat, dissolve the sugar and water and add the glucose.
2. Boil the mixture, stirring constantly, until the mixture reaches 245°F, or until the mixture forms a firm ball when tested in cold water.
3. Remove the pan from the heat, and add the almonds and almond flavouring.
4. Carefully turn the mixture out onto a marble slab, or other heat safe work surface.
5. When the mixture is cool enough to handle, knead until smooth. Dust your hands and work surface with the icing sugar to prevent the marzipan becoming sticky.
6. You can shape the marzipan into anything you like. Store somewhere cool.

Q. Is there a marzipan recipe I can try which uses eggs?

A. Yes. This recipe for rich marzipan uses eggs. You can choose to use either egg whites or yolks. Using egg yolks will give your marzipan a slightly richer flavour.

RICH MARZIPAN

INGREDIENTS

1 lb sugar
3 cups ground almonds
2 egg whites, or 2 egg yolks
½ cup water
1 tbsp glucose
1 lb shop-bought fondant

METHOD

1. In a heavy-bottomed saucepan dissolve the sugar in the water, then add the glucose and heat the mixture until the thermometer reads 240°F, or until the mixture forms a soft ball when tested in cold water.

2. Remove the pan from the heat, and stir in the almonds.

3. The paste should be fairly stiff at this point.

4. When the mixture has cooled slightly, add the beaten egg whites, or beaten egg yolks and heat gently until the mixture won't adhere to the sides of the pan.

5. Remove the pan from the heat and carefully pour the mixture onto a marble slab, or other heat safe work surface.

6. When the mixture is cool enough to handle, knead until smooth.

7. Lay the marzipan out onto baking parchment, and leave it to stand somewhere cool for 24 hours before using.

Q. Is there a recipe for marzipan which I can make and use at a later date?

A. Yes. This recipe for make-up-and-use later marzipan is a handy addition, and rather simple to make, too.

MAKE UP AND USE LATER MARZIPAN

INGREDIENTS

2 cups ground almonds
¾ lb flavoured fondant
2 cups sugar
1/2 cup water
1 ½ tbsp glucose
⅛ tsp flavouring or extract (optional)
⅛ tsp food colouring (optional)

METHOD

1. In a large bowl, rub the almonds into the fondant with a wooden spoon.
2. In a heavy-bottomed saucepan, dissolve the sugar in the water over a low heat.
3. Add the glucose, and without stirring heat the mixture to 250°F, or until the mixture forms a hard ball when tested in cold water.
4. Quickly add the contents of the saucepan to the almond and fondant mixture and stir until the mixture begins to harden.
5. Carefully turn the mixture out onto a smooth work surface, and knead until smooth.
6. Add the extract and flavouring to the dough while it is still warm.
7. Wrap the marzipan in baking parchment, and then a clean cloth to store.

*Note. A few drops of lukewarm water can be added to the marzipan to soften it up before use.

Q. Can you use honey when making marzipan sweets?

A. Yes, honey was traditionally used to make marzipan as a substitute for sugar, when sugar was more scarce than it is nowadays. Here's a great recipe for honey marzipan you can try at home.

HONEY MARZIPAN SWEETS

INGREDIENTS

2 cups almonds
1 tbsp caster sugar
2 tbsp clear runny honey
1 tbsp lemon juice
1 tbsp icing sugar, to dust

METHOD

1. Put the almonds and caster sugar into a food processor and pulse until the mixture resembles coarse breadcrumbs. Do not over-process, otherwise the nuts may release their oils and become greasy. Drizzle in the honey and lemon juice and blend until the mixture starts to clump together.

2. Turn the marzipan onto a smooth work surface dusted with icing sugar and knead lightly until your mixture is soft and smooth.

3. Roll your marzipan out flat to a thickness of about ¼" and cut into small squares.

4. Store somewhere cool.

Q. Can you add fruit to marzipan sweets?

A. Yes, fruit works wonderfully in marzipan. Try this recipe for cherry marzipan balls.

CHERRY MARZIPAN BALLS

INGREDIENTS

½ cup confectioners' sugar
½ granulated sugar
2 cups ground almonds
1 cup chopped glace cherries
2 egg whites
¼ tsp cherry flavouring
¼ tsp red colouring

METHOD

1. In a large bowl, sift together the sugar, then add the almonds and mix well.

2. Beat the egg whites until they are frothy, and fold them into the sugar and almond mixture.

3. Add the extract and colouring, and knead well to create a stiff paste. Add a little extra sugar if the mixture is too wet.

4. Sprinkle the chopped cherries onto your work surface, and roll the mixture over them. Blend the cherries into the marzipan mixture by kneading well.

5. Allow the mixture to stand for a few hours, then shape into bite-sized balls by hand.

6. Use the marzipan as soon as possible as it won't store for longer than 24 hours.

Q. Can you use fruit other than cherries?

A. Yes, you can use any of your favourite dried fruits. Here is a recipe recipe for raisin marzipan sweets.

RAISIN MARZIPAN

INGREDIENTS

4 tbsp raisins
1 egg white
¾ cup ground almonds
⅓ cup confectioners' sugar
½ tsp rose extract
¼ tsp almond extract
⅛ tsp red food colouring
½ cup icing sugar, for dusting

METHOD

1. In a large bowl, beat the egg white until it is stiff, and then sift in the confectioners' sugar.

2. Add the almonds, raisins, extracts and colouring to the egg white and sugar and mix well until the mixture takes on a dough-like consistency.

3. Carefully turn the mixture out onto a smooth work surface dusted with icing sugar.

4. Dust a rolling pin with a little icing sugar, and roll the mixture out to about ¼" thick.

5. Use small cookie cutters to shape your marzipan.

Q. Can you use citrus fruits in marzipan sweets?

A. Yes, citrus fruits work well in marzipan sweets. This unusual recipe for lemon marzipan, or manzapades, is a traditional Jewish treat which originates from Greece. You can even get creative and mold the marzipan into mini lemon-shaped sweets.

LEMON MARZIPAN OR MANZAPADES

INGREDIENTS

The dried lemon peels of 12 lemons
1 cup blanched almonds, finely ground
2 cups granulated sugar
1 cup icing sugar

METHOD

1. Put the lemon peels in a bowl, and cover them with water. Leave them to soak for two days, changing the water every 3-4 hours.

2. On the third day, rinse the peels and put them into a large saucepan with water to cover. Place over low heat and simmer for 45 to 60 minutes, until peels are very soft.

3. Remove the pan from the heat and pulse the peel in a food processor. You should have about one cup of pulp.

4. Return the pulp to the large saucepan and add the ground almonds and granulated sugar. Mix well and place over a low heat. Stir often with a wooden spoon. Cook until the mixture thickens and starts peeling away from the pan sides.

5. Remove the pan from the heat and pour onto a marble slab or other smooth work surface.

6. When the mixture has cooled slightly, spread the powdered sugar onto a separate plate. Knead the mixture a little and then pinch off pieces the size of hazelnuts. Roll them into balls and then roll in the powdered sugar.

7. Allow the marzipan to rest for 24 hours before serving.

Q. Are there any recipes for citrus fruit marzipan which don't require so much preparation?

A. Yes, this recipe for little marzipan oranges is much simpler to prepare but still has an unmistakably zingy flavour.

MARZIPAN ORANGES

INGREDIENTS

2 cups caster sugar
2 cups icing sugar, plus extra for dusting
3 cups ground almonds
Grated zest and juice 1 orange
1 egg
1 egg yolk
Cloves, to decorate (optional)

METHOD

1. In a large bowl, sift the sugar and almonds together, then stir in the orange zest.
2. Beat together the egg and egg yolk and add to the sugar mixture, stirring well.
3. Carefully turn the mixture out onto a smooth work surface and knead well.
4. Add a little orange juice if the mix is too dry, or icing sugar if too wet.
5. Shape small amounts of marzipan into oranges, rolling them over a zest grater to give a textured finish. You can add a clove as a stalk to make them look even more realistic.
6. Store somewhere cool.

Q. Can you use nuts other than almonds when making marzipan sweets?

A. Yes, lots of nuts can be used to make marzipan sweets, although almonds are most commonly used. Try this recipe for cashew marzipan which is a traditional Indian sweet called Kaju Barfi.

KAJU BARFI

INGREDIENTS

3 cups sugar
1 cup water
5 cups ground cashew nuts
¼ tsp orange flavouring
¼ tsp colouring

METHOD

1. In a large saucepan, dissolve the sugar and water and add the cashews.
2. Heat the mixture gently, stirring constantly, until the mass will not adhere to the pan.
3. Remove the pan from the heat and carefully pour the mixture onto a marble slab, or other heat safe work surface.
4. When the mixture is cool enough to handle, knead until smooth, adding the colouring and flavouring while the mixture is still warm.
5. Roll out to about ½" thickness.
6. Cut into bite-sized squares. Store somewhere cool.

Q. What other nuts can be used as a base when making marzipan sweets?

A. This recipe for pistachio marzipan is great, and the bright green nuts will give your sweets a vibrant pop of colour.

PISTACHIO MARZIPAN SWEETS

INGREDIENTS

2 cups shelled unsalted pistachios
1 tbsp caster sugar
2 tbsp clear runny honey
1 tbsp lemon juice
1 tbsp icing sugar, to dust

METHOD

1. Put the pistachio nuts and caster sugar into a food processor and pulse until the mixture resembles coarse breadcrumbs. Drizzle in the honey and lemon juice and blend until the mixture starts to clump together.
2. Turn the marzipan onto a smooth work surface dusted with icing sugar and knead lightly until your mixture is soft and smooth.
3. Take small pieces of mixture and roll them into balls.
4. Dust with a little icing sugar, and store somewhere cool.

Q. Parzipan is mentioned earlier in this book. Is there a recipe I can try at home?

A. Yes, try this recipe for traditional peach or apricot kernel-based marzipan.

PARZIPAN

INGREDIENTS

1 lb sugar
3 cups ground peach or apricot kernels
2 egg whites, or 2 egg yolks
½ cup water
1 tbsp glucose
¼ tsp choice flavouring

METHOD

1. In a heavy-bottomed saucepan dissolve the sugar in the water, then add the glucose and heat the mixture until the thermometer reads 240°F, or until the mixture forms a soft ball when tested in cold water.

2. Remove the pan from the heat, and stir in the almonds. The paste should be fairly stiff at this point.

3. When the mixture has cooled slightly, add the beaten egg whites, or beaten egg yolks and heat gently until the mixture won't adhere to the sides of the pan.

4. Remove the pan from the heat and carefully pour the mixture onto a marble slab, or other heat-safe work surface.

5. When the mixture is cool enough to handle, knead until smooth.

6. Take small pieces of the mixture and shape into small balls. Roll the balls in icing sugar, and store somewhere cool.

Q. Is it possible to make nut-free marzipan sweets?

A. Yes, try this simple recipe for nut-free marzipan, which ingeniously uses semolina as a substitute for almonds meal. This recipe uses the subtle flavour of orange flower water, but you can add any flavours you like.

NUT-FREE MARZIPAN

INGREDIENTS

5 oz icing sugar
5 oz semolina
2 tsp custard powder
1 egg white, beaten
2 tsp orange flower water,
or other essence of your choice

METHOD

1. Sift the icing sugar into a large bowl, and add the semolina and custard powder.
2. Add the beaten egg white to the mixture and stir well with a wooden spoon.
3. Add the extract of your choice and mix until the mixture forms a rough dough.
4. Turn the mixture out onto a smooth work surface, and knead well.
5. Take small pieces of the mixture and form them into balls.
6. Roll the sweets in icing sugar, and store somewhere cool.

Q. Can you add liqueur to marzipan?

A. Yes, liqueur works well as a flavour in marzipan, especially a nut-based liqueur like Amaretto, or Frangelico. Try this recipe for double almond marzipan sweets, which is a perfect gift for adults.

DOUBLE ALMOND MARZIPAN

INGREDIENTS

3 cups sugar
5 cups ground almonds
1 cup water
1 tbsp Amaretto
½ cup icing sugar

METHOD

1. In a heavy-bottomed saucepan dissolve the sugar and water over a low heat.
2. Add the almonds, and stir until the mixture won't adhere to the sides of the pan.
3. Carefully turn the mixture out onto a marble slab or other heatsafe work surface.
4. When the mixture is cool enough to handle, knead well.
5. Make a well in the middle of your ball of kneaded mixture, and gradually pour in the Amaretto, kneading the marzipan to blend.
6. If the marzipan mixture is too wet, add a little icing sugar as you knead. If the mixture is too dry, add a drop more Amaretto.
7. Take small pieces of marzipan and roll into bite-sized balls.
8. Dust the balls with icing sugar, and store somewhere cool.

Q. What else can you flavour marzipan sweets with?

A. Vanilla works wonderfully as a flavour in marzipan, as the sweetness complements the distinctive flavour of almonds perfectly.

VANILLA MARZIPAN

INGREDIENTS

2 cups golden caster sugar
3 cups icing sugar
(plus a little extra for kneading and rolling out)
4 cups ground almonds
seeds scraped from 1 vanilla pod
2 eggs, beaten
½ tsp orange or lemon juice

METHOD

1. In a large bowl, mix the sugars and almonds with a wooden spoon, then add the vanilla seeds and stir well.
2. Make a well in the middle, and add the eggs and citrus juice.
3. Use a knife to cut the dry ingredients into the wet, until the mixture starts to form a rough dough.
4. Turn the mixture out onto a smooth work surface, dusted with a little icing sugar.
5. Knead the marzipan until smooth and the ingredients are well blended.
6. Shape the mixture into little balls and roll them in a little more icing sugar.
7. Store somewhere cool.

Q. Can you flavour marzipan with coffee?

A. Yes, try this recipe for coffee and walnut marzipan bites. These sweets use walnut meats for decoration and are the perfect coffee break treat.

COFFEE AND WALNUT MARZIPAN BITES

INGREDIENTS

¼ lb Cooked Marzipan
1 shot of espresso/ ½ cup strong coffee
1 cup walnut meats

METHOD

1. Dust a smooth work surface with icing sugar, and start kneading your cooked marzipan.

2. While it is still a ball, make a well in the marzipan and carefully pour in the coffee. You will have to do this gradually, or the coffee will not be absorbed by the marzipan.

3. Carefully knead the marzipan, blending the coffee into the mixture.

4. Form small balls out of your coffee marzipan, and press two walnut halves onto the sides.

5. Serve straightaway.

Q. Can you make fruit-flavoured marzipan sweets?

A. Yes, fruit flavours work well with marzipan. You can also get creative and shape your marzipan into miniature pieces of fruit. These make perfect presents, and can also be used to decorate cakes or desserts.

STRAWBERRY MARZIPAN

INGREDIENTS

½ cup confectioners' sugar
½ granulated sugar
2 cups ground almonds
2 egg whites
¼ tsp strawberry flavouring
⅛ tsp green food colouring
¼ tsp red food colouring
Cloves, to decorate

METHOD

1. In a large bowl, sift together the sugar, then add the almonds and mix well.

2. Beat the egg whites until they are frothy, and fold them into the sugar and almond mixture.

3. Remove a small amount of mixture and add the green colouring to it. Knead well to blend the colour through the marzipan.

4. Add the extract and red colouring to the remaining mixture and knead well to create a stiff paste. Add a little extra sugar if the mixture is too wet.

5. Allow the mixture to stand for a few hours, then shape into strawberries (see pg 84).

6. Use the marzipan as soon as possible as it won't store for longer than 24 hours.

*See the next page for how to shape the strawberries.

TO SHAPE THE STRAWBERRIES

1. Roll small pieces of marzipan into balls and pinch at one end to create a strawberry-shaped sweet.

2. Take the green marzipan and roll it to a thickness of about ¼" with a rolling pin.

3. Use a sharp knife to cut star-shaped pieces of marzipan to use as the strawberry hulls.

4. Roll the strawberry-shaped sweets over a zest grater to create a textured finish.

5. Place the green hulls onto the sweets, and pin them into place with a clove 'stalk'.

Q. Can you make sweets with just a hint of marzipan?

A. This recipe for stuffed prunes is great if you want just a little taste of marzipan. Prunes are the perfect size to stuff, and once pitted, have a ready-made cavity which is perfect for stuffing.

STUFFED PRUNES

INGREDIENTS

1 cup prunes
⅛ lb Cooked Marzipan
2 cups sugar
½ cup water
¼ tsp cream of tartar
½ cup chopped coconut or chopped pistachio nuts

METHOD

1. Stone the prunes, and carefully fill the cavity with marzipan.
2. In a heavy-bottomed saucepan, dissolve the sugar in the water.
3. Add the cream of tartar and heat the mixture until it reaches 290°F, or the mixture forms firm, flexible strands when tested in cold water.
4. Leave the mixture to cool slightly, then carefully dip each prune into the syrup.
5. Roll the prunes in the coconut or pistachio, and leave to dry on a plate somewhere cool.

Q. I know marzipan is often used as a topping on Christmas cake, but is there a recipe I can use to make Christmas marzipan sweets?

A. Yes, these cute little marzipan Christmas puddings are a fantastic Christmas treat, and carefully wrapped, would make a fantastic gift.

MARZIPAN CHRISTMAS PUDDINGS

INGREDIENTS

½ cup confectioners' sugar
½ cup granulated sugar
2 cups ground almonds
2 egg whites
1 tsp grated nutmeg
2 tbsp dried cranberries, finely chopped.

METHOD

1. In a large bowl, sift together the sugar, then add the almonds and mix well.
2. Beat the egg whites until they are frothy, and fold them into the sugar and almond mixture.
3. Add the cranberries, and knead well to create a stiff paste. Add a little extra sugar if the mixture is too wet.
4. Allow the mixture to stand for a few hours, then shape small pieces of the marzipan into balls.
5. Sprinkle the grated nutmeg onto a plate, and carefully roll the balls in it to create a mottled, speckled finish.
6. Use the marzipan as soon as possible as it won't store for longer than 24 hours.

TOP TEN TIPS

PREPARATION

1. Buy a thermometer. It will make your marzipan-making a lot simpler, and much more accurate.

2. Make sure you 'break in' a new thermometer. Put the thermometer into a pan of cold water, bring the pan to the boil, and leave it there until the water has cooled.

3. After using your thermometer to test the temperature, plunge it into warm water and wipe it straight away.

4. Have all your ingredients measured and ready before you begin. Marzipan making is very precise, and having everything ready will ensure nothing is overcooked.

5. Follow the recipe exactly. Until you have a lot of marzipan-making experience, it is best to follow recipes exactly. When you become more confident, you can experiment with your own variations.

AND TRICKS

MARZIPAN SWEETS

6. Once you have poured the mixture out of the pan, immediately fill it with hot water and return it to the heat for a few minutes. This will stop your mixture setting onto the pan and will make it a lot easier to clean.

7. Take your marzipan out of the fridge at least five minutes before using it to ensure it won't be too hard to work with.

8. Dust your hands and your work surface with icing sugar when working with marzipan. This will stop your marzipan becoming too sticky.

9. Marzipan does not stay fresh for very long, so make sure you make it as near to when you need to use it as possible.

10. Marzipan is best stored in an airtight container in the fridge.

TOP TEN TIPS

SHAPING M

1. Get creative and add texture to your sweets. If you are shaping marzipan into miniature fruits, think about the kind of texture you want to achieve.

2. Rolling your sweets over a zest grater will give a wonderful texture, or you could try running a fork or serrated knife over the surface of your sweets.

3. Small cookie cutters are a quick and easy way to shape your marzipan sweets. Roll your marzipan to about ¼" thick first.

4. Liquorice is useful when decorating your marzipan sweets, as it can be used to adorn fruit and vegetable-shaped marzipan, as stalks for example.

5. Cloves are useful, and can be used to mimic stalks for your marzipan fruit. Just be sure to remove them before you eat your sweets!

6. Kneading food colouring through your marzipan is an easy way of getting a smooth, even colour to your sweets.

AND TRICKS

CRAFTING

7. Painting colouring on with a fine paintbrush allows you to achieve an intricate finish to your marzipan sweets.

8. A cocktail stick is a handy tool, and can be used to create texture , or add detail to the surface of your sweets.

9. Dusting your sweets with ground spices is an easy way to add colour as well as flavour to your marzipan. Cinnamon and nutmeg work well with marzipan and gently rolling your sweets over a mixture of spices and sugar creates a wonderfully mottled effect.

10. Using real leaves, cloves, or small herbs to adorn your marzipan sweets can be really effective. Just remember to remove them before you enjoy them!

NOTES

NOTES

Image Credits

All Pages - This work is a derivative of "Textures: Paper IMG_0006" is Copyright ©2007-2012 ~Dioma, made available on DeviantArt under Creative Commons Attribution 2.0 Generic (CC BY 2.0) http://dioma.deviantart.com/art/Textures-Paper-58028330

All Pages - This work is a derivative of "Textures: Paper IMG_0002" is Copyright ©2007-2012 Dioma, made available on DeviantArt under Creative Commons Attribution 2.0 Generic (CC BY 2.0) http://dioma.deviantart.com/art/Textures-Paper-58028330

All Chapter Pages - This work is a derivative of "Frame back" is copyright © 2009 Sunset Sailor made available on Flickr under Creative Commons Attribution 2.0 Generic (CC BY 2.0) http://www.flickr.com/photos/sunsetsailor/3558408492

Page 2-3 - This work is a derivative of "Marzipan Cakes" is copyright © 2012 Adrian Fu, made available on Flickr under Creative Commons Attribution 2.0 Generic (CC BY 2.0) http://www.flickr.com/photos/adrian-fu/7930572172/

Pages 6-7 - This work is a derivative of "OHM_-_Marzipanmodel 2.jpg" is copyright © 2010 By Wolfgang Sauber, made available on Wikimedia Commons, GNU Free Documentation License, http://commons.wikimedia.org/wiki/File%3AOHM_-_Marzipanmodel_2.jpg

Pages 19 - This work is a derivative of "Autumn red peach.jpg" is copyright © Date Not given Transferred by Fæ on 2013-02-27, Jack Dykinga, U.S. Department of Agriculture, made available on Wikimedia Commons, under public domain licence http://commons.wikimedia.org/wiki/File:Autumn_red_peach.jpg

Page 20-21 This work is a derivative of "Pots and Pans" is copyright © 2012 jeeheon made available on Flickr under Creative Commons Attribution 2.0 Generic (CC BY 2.0) http://www.flickr.com/photos/jeeheon/7877017204

Page 29 - This work is a derivative of "Cutting ginger snaps.jpg" is copyright © 2005 BenFrantzDale, made available on Wikimedia Commons, under Creative Commons Attribution 3.0 Generic (CC BY 3.0) http://commons.wikimedia.org/wiki/File:Cutting_ginger_snaps.jpg#file

Pages 30-31 - This work is a derivative of "Kitchen Tools at the Table" is copyright © 2012, slightly everything, Kate Hiscock, made available on Flickr under Creative Commons Attribution 2.0 Generic (CC BY 2.0) http://www.flickr.com/photos/slightlyeverything/8229722025

Page 46-47 - This work is a derivative of "Making Almond Meal By Hand" is copyright © 2007 goosmurf, Yun Huang Yong, made available on Flickr under Creative Commons Attribution 3.0 Generic (CC BY 2.0) http://www.flickr.com/photos/goosmurf/2154523790/in/photostream/

Pages 58-59 - This work is a derivative of "Marzipan" is copyright © 2012 aurélien., Aurelien Guichard, made available on Flickr under Creative Commons Attribution 2.0 Generic (CC BY 2.0) http://www.flickr.com/photos/aguichard/8311107161/

Pages 85 - This work is a derivative of "Marzipan Fruits" is copyright © 2012 andybullock77, Andy Bullock, made available on Flickr under Creative Commons Attribution 2.0 Generic (CC BY 2.0) http://www.flickr.com/photos/aguichard/8311107161/

www.ingramcontent.com/pod-product-compliance
Lightning Source LLC
Chambersburg PA
CBHW050114170426
43198CB00014B/2572